W9-AHX-752

Searchlight
BOOKS™

What
Can We
Learn from Early
Civilizations?

Tools and Treasures of

Ancient
Greece

Matt Doeden

Lerner Publications Company
Minneapolis

Lerner Publications Company
A division of Lerner Publishing Group, Inc.
241 First Avenue North
Minneapolis, MN 55401 U.S.A.

For reading levels and more information, look up this title at www.lernerbooks.com.

Library of Congress Cataloging-in-Publication Data

Doeden, Matt.
    Tools and treasures of ancient Greece / by Matt Doeden.
        pages   cm. — (Searchlight books™ : what can we learn from early civilizations?)
    Includes index.
    ISBN 978–1–4677–1430–3 (lib. bdg. : alk. paper)
    ISBN 978–1–4677–2506–4 (eBook)
    1. Greece—Civilization—To 146 BCE—Juvenile literature. 2. Greece—Juvenile
literature. I. Title.
    DF77.D66 2014
    938—dc23   2013017735

Manufactured in the United States of America
1 – PC – 12/31/13

Contents

Chapter 1

THE ANCIENT GREEKS

More than twenty-five hundred years ago, ancient Greece was becoming a great civilization. The ancient Greeks had gifted artists, deadly warriors, and great thinkers. They also had an unusual government. It was the world's first real democracy. In a democracy, free people get to vote on their leaders and many of their laws.

Athens is the capital city of modern-day Greece. Ancient Athens was the birthplace of democracy. What is a democracy?

Ancient Greece changed the world. It shaped many cultures that followed it. The Greeks left behind all sorts of useful tools and amazing treasures.

Beautiful art is just one of many treasures to come from ancient Greece.

Rugged Land

Ancient Greece was in southeastern Europe. It sat on the tip of the Balkan Peninsula. This part of Europe sticks out into the Mediterranean Sea. The land is rough and covered with mountains.

Greece's rocky land once made farming and traveling difficult.

Greece was made up of many city-states. Each city-state had its own leaders and laws. Two of the largest city-states were Athens and Sparta.

These ruins were once a large theater in Sparta.

Early in Greek history, people rarely visited other city-states. Traveling on foot or horseback was hard. But Greece was surrounded on three sides by water. Many Greeks were expert sailors and traveled by sea.

These people are restoring an ancient Greek trading ship so it will look new again.

Ancient Greece

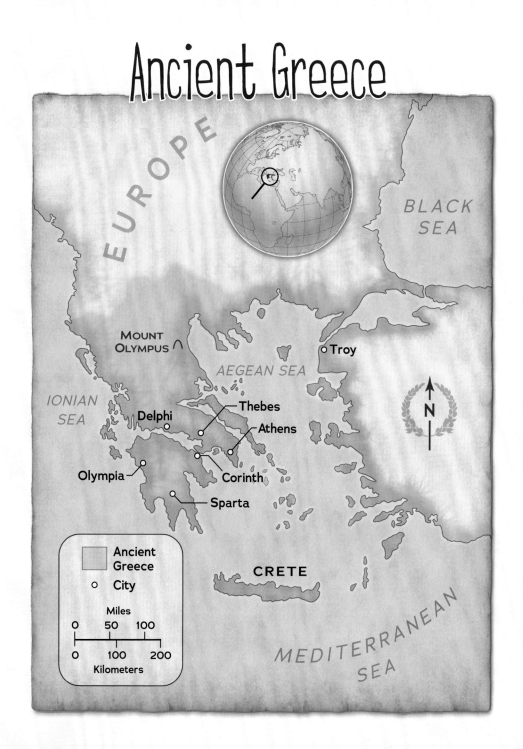

EUROPE

BLACK SEA

MOUNT OLYMPUS ⋀

Troy

AEGEAN SEA

IONIAN SEA

Delphi

Thebes

Athens

N

Olympia

Corinth

Sparta

☐ Ancient Greece

○ City

Miles
0   50   100

0   100   200
Kilometers

CRETE

MEDITERRANEAN SEA

Around 500 BCE, Persia tried to take over Greece. The city-states joined together to defend themselves. They held back the Persian army. The city-states also formed a common culture. That's how the golden age of ancient Greece began.

The Greeks defeated the Persians in the Battle of Salamis in 480 BCE. This painting from the 1900s shows the battle.

Chapter 2

DAILY LIFE

Free Greek men spent most of their time in public. They gathered to talk about art and science. They voted on laws. They threw parties and went to the theater.

Ancient Greeks often met to share ideas. This painting from the 1500s shows how their meetings might have looked. What topics did Greek men discuss?

Most Greek women weren't allowed to join these activities. They stayed home. They did housework and raised children. Some couldn't even go outside! But women in Sparta had more rights. They studied the arts. They played sports. They even helped the men run Sparta's government.

Greek women stayed in their houses. This woman is putting clothes into a large chest.

Some men and women were slaves. They worked in the homes of free Greeks. They cooked, made clothes, and did other chores. Slaves had little control over their lives. They had to do whatever their owners told them. And slaves got no pay. Some Greeks treated their slaves very harshly. Young warriors in Sparta killed slaves as part of their training.

Some slaves were children. This work of art shows a young slave (LEFT) and his owner (RIGHT).

Work

Many ancient Greeks were farmers. They grew wheat, barley, olives, figs, grapes, and more. Farmers also raised animals such as goats, sheep, pigs, and chickens.

OLIVE TREE FIELDS STILL GROW IN GREECE.

Some Greeks were fishers. Others were builders, artists, or teachers. A few freemen in each city-state were in charge of the government. Other men chose them to make most of the laws.

Greeks used these iron tools in everyday life.

War was common. So most men spent at least some time training as soldiers. All free Spartan men were full-time soldiers! They started training at the age of seven. Soldiers carried long spears and shields. The Greeks also used bows and arrows, short swords, and javelins.

Weapons of war often appear on ancient Greek pottery. This bowl shows the goddess Artemis with a bow and arrows.

Communication

The language of ancient Greece was a lot like the modern Greek language. The Greek alphabet has twenty-four letters, from alpha to omega. Modern Greeks still use this alphabet. Every other European alphabet is based on it.

Which letters in the Greek alphabet look familiar?

A	B	Γ	Δ	E	Z	H	Θ	I
ALPHA	BETA	GAMMA	DELTA	EPSILON	ZETA	ETA	THETA	IOTA
a	b	g	d	ě	ds	ē	th	i

K	Λ	M	N	Ξ	O	Π	P
KAPPA	LAMBDA	MU	NU	XSI	OMICRON	PI	RHO
k	l	m	n	x	ŏ	p	r

Σ	T	Y	Φ	X	Ψ	Ω
SIGMA	TAU	UPSILON	PHI	CHI	PSI	OMEGA
s	t	ü	ph	ch(k)	ps	ō

αβγδεζηθικλμνξοπρσςτυφχψω

a   b   g   d   ě   ds   ē   th   i   k   l   m   n   x   ŏ   p   r   s   s   t   ü   ph   ch   ps   ō
                                                                          *   (k)

αβγδεζηθικλμνξοπρσςτυφχψω

ʹ ʹ ʹ ʹ ʹ ʹ ʹ ʹ ʹ ʹ ʹ ʹ ~ - ..

only and always used at end of word.

The Greeks wrote on tablets made of wood or leather. The tablets were covered with wax. Greeks used a writing tool called a stylus to form the letters. The Greeks used writing in many ways. They kept track of harvests. They wrote stories about heroes and gods. They even sent letters to one another.

Writing lessons in ancient Athens might have looked like this.

Religion

The Greeks believed gods controlled Earth. The gods had great powers. But they were also a lot like people. They usually looked human. They fought, fell in love, and played tricks.

Athena was the goddess of warfare and wisdom.

The Greeks wanted to keep their gods happy. They hoped the gods would protect them from disease, bad weather, and war.

So the Greeks built temples to honor the gods. People prayed there. They also offered food and animals as sacrifices. The most famous ancient Greek temple is the Parthenon in Athens.

Modern tourists can still visit the Parthenon.

Chapter 3

THE CULTURE OF ANCIENT GREECE

No ancient culture had a bigger impact on the modern world than ancient Greece. Its art and architecture still affect modern styles. Its thinkers changed the way people saw the world. And its government is a model for modern democracies.

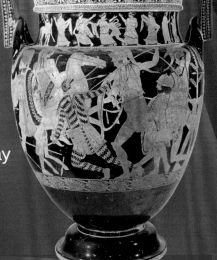

Greek art styles influence modern art. In what other ways did ancient Greece impact the modern world?

Art

Ancient Greeks valued many art forms. Artists painted on walls, wood panels, and pottery. Sculptors used metal tools to carve images into stone or metal. One of the greatest Greek sculptures was a statue of the god Zeus. It was 42 feet (13 meters) tall. That's about as tall as a four-story building!

The statue of Zeus was destroyed in the 500s CE. But this is how it might have looked.

The Greeks loved plays. Actors performed in outdoor theaters. The Greeks invented the main types of plays that are still common today. Tragedies had sad endings. Comedies ended happily.

THE MASK OF TRAGEDY, WHICH THE MAN IN THIS SCULPTURE IS HOLDING, IS STILL USED IN MANY THEATERS.

Music was another common art form. It was played at important events. But people also played it for fun. Greek musicians had many instruments. The panpipe was a kind of flute. A lyre was a stringed instrument. The Greeks even had trumpets.

Greek musicians played the lyre (LEFT) and the panpipe (RIGHT).

Architecture

Most buildings in ancient Greece were made of bricks formed from sunbaked mud. But temples were made of stone. Stone is a strong material. It lasts a long time. So some ancient Greek temples are still standing! These buildings had a simple, graceful style. Tall columns held up the roofs. This design later became popular all around Europe.

These ancient Greek columns stand in the city of Corinth.

The Greeks also built huge outdoor theaters. Most theaters stood on a slope. The stage was at the bottom. Rows of seats lined the slope. This design made it easy for everyone to see the stage.

How are ancient Greek theaters like modern-day movie theaters?

Sports

The ancient Greeks loved sports. Young men wrestled, boxed, ran races, and competed in the long jump. They threw the javelin and the discus. The Greeks even invented a 26-mile (42-kilometer) footrace called a marathon.

Wrestling was a popular sport for young Greek men.

The Greeks held the first Olympic Games in 776 BCE. These games were very different from the modern Olympics. Only free Greek men could compete. The winners' prizes were wreaths made from olive branches.

The 2004 Olympic Games took place in Athens. In a nod to tradition, winning athletes wore olive wreaths.

The Flight of Icarus

The ancient Greeks had many myths. Each myth explained a belief or taught a lesson. One tale tells of a boy named Icarus who ignored an important warning.

Icarus was the son of Daedalus, a master craftsman. Daedalus and Icarus were prisoners on the island of Crete. But Daedalus came up with a plan to escape. He used feathers and wax to build two pairs of wings. He and Icarus strapped the wings to their backs so they could fly away.

"Follow me," Daedalus told Icarus. "Don't fly too high."

Icarus and his father took off into the sky. Icarus was thrilled that he could fly. He grew careless and kept flying higher. It grew hotter and hotter as he flew closer to the sun. Soon the heat melted the wax in his wings. The wings fell apart. Icarus dropped to his death in the sea below.

Chapter 4

THE FALL OF ANCIENT GREECE

Greece was strongest when its city-states worked together against a common enemy. But Greece and Persia made peace in 449 BCE. Then the Greek city-states fought among themselves.

This helmet is from the ancient Greek city-state of Corinth. How did Greece change when the city-states started fighting one another?

Athens and Sparta fought each other in the Peloponnesian War (431–404 BCE). It lasted twenty-six years! Sparta finally won. But the long struggle weakened all of Greece.

This is a replica of an ancient Greek warship.

The Spartans didn't hold power for long. King Philip II of Macedon took over during the 350s BCE. His son, Alexander, replaced him in 336 BCE.

During Philip II's rule, his face appeared on Greek coins.

Alexander was a great military leader. His armies conquered Persia, Egypt, India, and many other lands. He controlled the biggest empire in the world. Greece had never been stronger.

STATUES OF ALEXANDER THE GREAT EXIST ALL OVER THE WORLD.

Alexander died in 323 BCE. His generals all wanted to rule in his place. So they fought one another for power. The empire was torn apart. The golden age of Greece was over.

Alexander never lost a battle. This image from ancient Rome shows him leading his army.

Enter the Romans

The weakened city-states survived for almost two hundred more years. But by 146 BCE, Rome had conquered Greece. Greece became part of the Roman Empire.

The Greek forces were no match for the Romans. These modern actors use replicas of Roman armor and weapons.

Greek culture didn't die out, though. The Romans copied Greek styles of art and building. They used Greek musical instruments. Their religion was based on Greek beliefs. Their government borrowed ideas from Greek democracy. The Romans spread these ideas all around Europe.

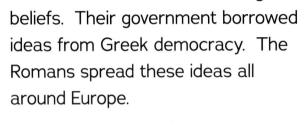

How does this statue of the Roman goddess Minerva look similar to the Greek goddess Athena (SHOWN ON PAGE 19)?

Greece Today

Descendants of the ancient Greeks still live in present-day Greece. The nation is home to about 11 million people. Athens is its capital. The city has changed a lot since the golden age. But many treasures of ancient Greece remain, from sculptures to writing to huge temples. They remind modern Greeks of the rich culture that thrived there thousands of years ago.

Ancient ruins stand alongside modern buildings in present-day Athens.

Glossary

city-state: a self-governing city and the lands it controls

civilization: a large society in which people share a common government and culture

conquer: to take over a land by force

democracy: a system of government in which citizens hold the power through voting, often via elected officials

discus: a thick, heavy disc thrown by athletes in the Olympics

empire: a large group of states or nations under a single leader

golden age: a period of time from about 500 to 323 BCE, when Greek culture and civilization was at its peak. This period is also called the classical age.

javelin: a light spear, used both in ancient combat and in throwing contests

marathon: a long running race that lasts 26 miles (42 km)

myth: a traditional story often told to teach a lesson or to explain something in nature

peninsula: a piece of land that juts out into an ocean or a sea

stylus: a tool used for writing

Learn More about Ancient Greece

Books

Cohn, Jessica. *The Ancient Greeks*. New York: Gareth Stevens, 2012. This fun book explores what everyday life was like in ancient Greece.

Fullman, Joe. *Ancient Greeks: Dress, Eat, Write and Play Just Like the Greeks*. Mankato, MN: QEB, 2010. Get a hands-on taste of ancient Greek culture with this activity-packed book.

Ganeri, Anita. *Ancient Greeks*. Mankato, MN: Stargazer Books, 2010. Find out how the ancient Greeks lived, which games they played, and what discoveries they made.

Levine, Michelle. *The Greeks: Life in Ancient Greece*. Minneapolis: Millbrook Press, 2010. Dig deeper to discover more about the first Olympics, early theaters, and other wonders of ancient Greece.

Websites

BBC Primary History—Ancient Greeks
http://www.bbc.co.uk/schools/primaryhistory/ancient_greeks
Do you wonder what it was like to grow up in ancient Greece? Are you curious about the Greek gods? Find the answers to your questions here!

Children's University—Ancient Greece
http://www.childrensuniversity.manchester.ac.uk/interactives/history/greece
Check out a timeline of ancient Greece, the Greek alphabet, games, and more!

HowStuffWorks—Ancient Greece
http://history.howstuffworks.com/ancient-greece
This website is packed with information on Greek history. Get the scoop on famous leaders and thinkers, important city-states, and much more.

LERNER

e

SOURCE

Expand learning beyond the printed book. Download free, complementary educational resources for this book from our website, www.lerneresource.com.

Index

Photo Acknowledgments

The images in this book are used with the permission of: © iStockphoto.com/kaetana_istock, p. 4; © Dshawley/ Dreamstime.com, p. 5; © iStockphoto.com/4allthingsweb, p. 6; © Hercules Milas/Alamy, p. 7; © Jonathan S. Blair/National Geographic/Getty Images, p. 8; © Laura Westlund/Independent Picture Service, p. 9; Album/Prisma/Newscom, p. 10; Wikimedia Commons, p. 11; © A young woman arranging her clothes in a coffer, 450 BC (stone), Greek, (5th century BC)/Museo Archeologico Nazionale, Taranto, Puglia, Italy/The Bridgeman Art Library, p. 12; © Young man with his slave, 430, BC funerary relief, Greek civilization, 5th Century BC/De Agostini Picture Library/G. Nimatallah/The Bridgeman Art Library, p. 13; © Andreas Karelias/Dreamstime.com, p. 14; © UIG via Getty Images, p. 15; © Attic red-figure bell krater (mixing bowl) Italy, said to be from Cumae, made in Athens, Early Classical Period, c.470 BC (pottery), Pan Painter (c.475-450 BC)/Museum of Fine Arts, Boston, Massachusetts, USA/James Fund and by Special Collection/The Bridgeman Art Library, p. 16; © iStockphoto.com/FreeTransform, p. 17; © Writing lesson in ancient Athens, Payne, Roger (b.1934)/Private Collection/© Look and Learn/The Bridgeman Art Library, p. 18; © DEA/G. NIMATALLAH/Getty Images, p. 19; © A.A.M. Van der Heyden/Independent Picture Service, p. 20; © SuperStock/Getty Images, p. 21; © The Statue of Olympian Zeus by Phidias, plate 5 from 'Entwurf einer historischen Architektur', engraved by Johann Adam Delsenbach (1687-1765) 1721 (engraving) (later colouration), Fischer von Erlach, Johann Bernhard (1656-1723) (after)/ Private Collection/The Stapleton Collection/The Bridgeman Art Library, p. 22; © Universal Images Group/Getty Images, p. 23; © Jgroup/Dreamstime.com, p. 24 (left); © Compuinfoto/Dreamstime.com, p. 24 (right); © John R. Kreul/Independent Picture Service, p. 25; © iStockphoto.com/yesfoto, p. 26; © The Wrestlers, after a Greek original of the 3rd century BC (marble) (b/w photo), Roman/Galleria degli Uffizi, Florence, Italy/ Alinari/The Bridgeman Art Library, p. 27; AP Photo/ DIETHER ENDLICHER, p. 28; © DEA/G. DAGLI ORTI/Getty Images, p. 29; © Corinthian Helmet, c.495 BC (bronze), Greek, (5th century BC)/Museum of Fine Arts, Houston, Texas, USA/Museum purchase/Funds provided by the Alice Pratt Brown Museum Fund/The Bridgeman Art Library, p. 30; © Replica of the trireme 'Olympia' at sea (photo)/Private Collection/Ancient Art and Architecture Collection Ltd./Mike Andrews/The Bridgeman Art Library, p. 31; © Bettmann/ CORBIS, p. 32; © iStockphoto.com/sneska, p. 33; © Araldo de Luca/CORBIS, p. 34; © Taylor S. Kennedy/National Geographic Society/CORBIS, p. 35; © Oleg Senkov/Shutterstock.com, p. 36; © Ddkg/Dreamstime.com, p. 37.

Front Cover: © DEA/G. DAGLI ORTI/Getty Images.

Main body text set in Adrianna Regular 14/20
Typeface provided by Chank